WHAT'S THE MATTER WITH TEXAS?

And The Resulting Red State Blues

By

Jim Green

DEDICATED TO:

Thomas Franks....and yes, this title borrows heavily from a fellow Kansan's query....to paraphrase "Why on God's earth would anyone in their right mind vote Republican—i.e., vote against their, and their children's economic well being?".....

ISBN-10:
1517715423

ISBN-13:
978-1517715427

PROLOGUE

And to expand briefly on the DEDICATION....we are a "representative" government—when we vote [in any rational scheme of things] we are voting for persons who will look out for the best economic interests of our selves and our family—we are voting for someone who has our back.....

And unless your last name is Koch or Walton [a metaphor, here, for the 1%]—The Republican party does not have your back---they *don't* represent *you*—indeed, the Republican party, today, has their hand in your pocket.....to even further enrich the Koch brothers! Not only did you vote against your own kid's well being—you are a sucker to boot!

And the Republicans are insufferable hypocrites....i.e., they have you chasing down blind alleys—in the name of "social values"—their policies undermine at every turn.....for instance, the House Republicans voted to cut $40 billion from Food Stamps [to gut the program] most of which goes to feed hungry children—children they demand women have, but are willing to starve to death, once born!

One of our top journalists, who shall remain nameless, nailed it: "the Republican Party, has become an insurgent outlier — ideologically extreme; contemptuous of the inherited social and economic policy regime; scornful of compromise; unpersuaded by conventional understanding of facts, evidence and science; and dismissive of the legitimacy of its political opposition.".

Also, compounding contemporary politics is a factor not given anywhere near the attention it should get—and that is electronic voting.

And as just one tiny example: If WalMart handed us a receipt for our purchases with the words "Trust Us" we would be outraged—but without a paper trail this is exactly what we have—but in this case, it is our democracy that is at stake!

The sad fact is, when 93% of Americans support background checks to screen out criminals and the mentally ill from purchasing a gun.....and the NRA was able to nullify the will of the American people—the belief that we are still a "democracy" is brought into serious question.......

And with hundred of millions of unaccounted for cash sloshing around—given the corrupt Citizens United decision—but surely no one would tamper with these machines, would they? Like does the sun rise in the East.....

In any event, and while we have a better chance of the sun coming up in the West—than our Republican controlled Congress to pass corrective legislation--proposed, here, is fail-safe electronic voting, to wit:

THE FAIL-SAFE ELECTRONIC VOTING ACT

EVERY electronic voting machine (hereafter EVM), must be inexpensive, identical throughout the U.S. in a 1/150 ratio, and *must count and produce a hard-copy of the recorded votes.* In addition, an extra copy of their recorded votes would be produced (not necessarily a hard-copy), marked "Voter's Copy", and containing "NOTICE: Do Not Destroy Until Every Election On Your Ballot Is Certified".

2) *After confirming that their votes are recorded correctly*, the voter would then insert the hard-copy ballot into a software-free (count only) optical scanner (hereafter OS), for a second count. The hard-copy ballot would be retained by election officials in the event a candidate asks for a recount (*not possible under the current system, and which undermines the legality of each such election)*. The EVM and the OS must be manufactured by different companies (which is universally true today).

3) Election officials assigned to oversee the EVM, would be prevented by law from overseeing the OS, and vice-versa, and stiff criminal penalties would be imposed for violations.

4) Further, every EVM would be programmed with raw data re the total registration rolls, by party, and norms for their voting history, etc.,----as an "alert" to a possible irregularity, such as an "under-vote"—or "vote-flipping" etc., and *standards* established to suspend certification where there is an "improbable result", at least temporarily,

of a particular election until the discrepancy is cleared up. (This is what computers do best, and it would be very easy to create such a program).

5) At the end of the election day, tallies would be taken from the EVM and the OS, for each election. *If the tallies didn't balance for any given election, or if there is an "alert", that election cannot be certified until the "error" is corrected.* If the candidates agree (the victory is certain), minor discrepancies in the count could be disregarded. While probably rare, the Voter, or a random sample of Voters, would be required by law to return their Copy of the recorded votes to the election office to clear up any "error", or where an "alert" signals the need for same.

6) Further, every state provides for a recount when the total vote falls below a certain percent of difference between the candidates, impossible to conduct with the current EVM. And thus Congress must mandate the following regarding presidential candidates: A RUN-OFF election is mandated and triggered in those states where the percent of total vote is less than .025% of difference between the two candidates; said election to be held on the second Saturday following the election, on PAPER BALLOTS ONLY/RED OR BLUE—with the voter chosing the color to vote on [for an easy recount], and contain ONLY the names of the relevant candidates, for instance: "Barack Obama, Democrat" and "John McCain, Republican"—with oversight in counting by a representative(s) of each party—said procedure providing more than adequate time to meet the Electoral College mandate [Ideally, all of this could be eliminated if we did away with the Electoral College, but until then....]. NOTE: Had this been the law in 2000, Al Gore would be our president, and America would have been spared the economic, etc., disaster that followed!

7) Finally, absent the above safeguards, and until these safeguards are in place--Congress must mandate that PAPER BALLOTS, ONLY, can be used in our presidential elections. This is not a "partisan" issue, it is a "pro-democracy" issue. Most importantly, this will return the responsibility for our elections, and our vote counting, back into the hands of the individual voter, where it belongs, and out of the hands of "corporate control"---*it is after all "our democracy", itself, that is at risk if we don't take these steps---and in that regard, is there any time or cost differential that is too great?*

Jim Green, Democrat candidate for Congress, 2000

Changing gears slightly--Singularly, the most perncicous "social" problem facing America, today, is *UNEMPLOYMENT*—and inexplicably we, as he larger society, have stepped aside and let the plutocracy/oligarchy write our policies [which not coincidentally have one foot on the plantation]—but this has also prevented our evolving in an ever-changing world economy, to wit:

OUR DILEMMA: The market is incapable of creating enough jobs to meet the demand—but our policies are based on the myth/lie, that it can—which has given rise to our insidious "social" problem of unemployment—under our current scheme if the market fails, the jobless are out of luck! And the primary purpose of this book is to explore this dilemma, and to propose a solution…..

If a mechanic is using a tool that will not fix the engine he is working on—should he go on using it because he wished it would work? That is the dilemma we face, today, in solving the pernicious consequences of unemployment—we stand on one foot and then the other wishing the market would solve a problem—it is INCAPABLE of solving….For instance, on this path, it has taken us 6 years to shave an anemic 4.9 points from our UE rate since the Great Meltdown.

When the Democrats were swept into office in 2009, and had majorities in the House, Senate and Presidency—having the Humphrey-Hawkins Full Employment Act, on the books, was like having a piece of gold in their hands—i.e., the "legal authorization" to limit our unemployment to "3%" permanently----indispensable in our current market economy--but they blew it….

The operative mind-set for job creation at the time, and since WW II—and driven by the obscene cash buying our elections, has been:

Fix the market, and this will fix unemployment—and when the mantra in the 2008 election—before the Great Meltdown was FIX UNEMPLOYMENT—it was obvious even before we were losing 700,000 thousands jobs per month, our model must change to "Fix unemployment, and this will fix the market"….

We simply must get over—get past—the ludicrous notion that ending our unemployment crisis—with public-sector jobs—is somehow communism, or socialism—or any other ism….

For those of us who lived through the McCarthy era—which caused millions of Americans to quake in fear that we had a "commie behind every tree"—the legacy still casts a shadow—and is paralyzing our evolving in a 21st market economy…. For instance, a blogger recently said that if the market didn't create work, well, there would be no work—and it went over his head that we have police, and librarians, and teachers…the larger point is that this paralyzing fear still casts a shadow lingers to this day with millions….

The fact is, and this will become more and more apparent the further we move into the 21st Century, that we have only one of two choices: To find work as the legal right of every citizen, or create a welfare system of some type. We have no other viable choices, and history has already shown us that welfare is more destructive, than constructive—but for the oligarchy, greed is always lingering in the background….

Greed is not inherent to capitalism—but it is too often an inevitable result…capitalism is build a better widget, sell it for a million bucks, and retire in Florida—nothing ignoble about that—the distinction seems best defined by using a medical model…..i.e., when a person enters the medical field as a means to get rich, rather than cure the ill—as related to the above……the reward is the pride one can take in making a better product…..

The unspoken, and yet most compelling question Americans face today, is: What do we pay for jointly, and what do we pay for individually? And overarching both is our creation of a good and decent society. Centuries ago, Cicero said "The common good is the highest law". The truth, however, is that the Republican Party, today, holds the Common Good in contempt! They want to do away with Social Security, and Food Stamps, and Planned Parenthood because they provide contraceptives, ad nauseam! In short, this current lot is a miserable excuse for human beings!

[An "Aha moment of clarity"--Texas is either under attack by the U.S. Army....Or....the Republican party is under attack by crazy people....Aha...now we know why the House is filled with lunatics who think obstructing President Obama [because he is black] is "a program", and why Ted Cruz was elected, and why Trump is making outlandish xenophobic statements to pander to our "crazy people"—to get their vote...their lunacy is endless....].....

But I digress.....

A few closing comments in the Prologue—As Oscar Wilde averred "The only truly worthless opinion is an unbiased one"—so bias, agreed—but always in the interest in getting at the larger goal—the truth....

Incidentally, I published my first book on my 78th birthday [I am currently 81]—and not that I write that fast, or well—the materials were all there for the better part of the past 30 years, give or take, gathering dust—it was just a matter of pulling them together in some order—also, don't believe any book should be over 60 pages, plus/minus— i.e., can be read in the crapper--two hours, max--lol—but it seems best summed up by a very astute observer [wish I could recall their name to give credit]: Persons who write do so because they have no choice [it is a compulsion, an addiction..]—they become an "author", however, when people start reading what they have written....

Finally, a note to the reader—the papers and letters are not in sequence, and apologize for redundancy [please look for the nuggets...Thx--lol]—also, if you are a "typo-wonk"—are more concerned with sentence structure, etc., than content—you probably won't like my writing—and you will find a wayward capital letter, here and there, and appearing out of place and used for emphasis—or a missing page...Hey, I'm and Indie....I chalk most up to editorial license and tongue-in-cheek, self-effacing humor—so apologies, here—[I seriously support: Take what you do seriously, but never yourself....]....

Just look for content, please....THX

CHAPTER ONE

O.J. SAMPSON
by
Jim Green

A futuristic fable, and blueprint for a safe and sane world following 9-11....

New Years Day, 2029

Word rippled like wildfire through the NFL grapevine, an elite group of past and present NFL football players O.J. Sampson (or just OJ, to his friends and the nation) had gotten into a violent marital dispute with his wife Michelle, the evening before, and OJ was arrested. Their marital difficulties were no secret to this group.

OJ stated that he would be making a public statement later that day....

How we had changed over the past forty years--grown up could perhaps best describe this change following the arrest and conviction of O.J. Simpson. It was ironic that Simpson had been arrested 40 years to the day earlier in a domestic dispute, on New Years Eve 1989--but no one heeded this red flag, and in 1996 Simpson was convicted of murdering his wife Nicole, and Ron Goldman, and Simpson was executed.

On the night of his execution, riots broke out in every major city in the United States--one quarter of Washington D.C was burned to the ground. With the fires clearly visible from the steps of the White House, President Clinton and the leaders of the Senate and House promised immediate legislative action--with major changes in the way we do business.

President Clinton proclaimed "Systemic problems, call for systemic solutions", and the following comprehensive legislative program, called: The Economic Inclusivism Act, was enacted into law within the next six months:

First, and long over due, the archaic terms "felony" and

"misdemeanor" were replaced in the classification of crime, and thereafter all crime was re-classified as either "violent" or "non-violent". The reason for this change was quite significant. The term "felony" was fixed in the public's mind as "armed and dangerous"...and yet, over 70% of our offenders were in prison for "non-violent" crimes...albeit all were "felons"! This distortion and distraction in terms stood in the way of our finding real solutions to the real problem: The violent offender. Indeed, in our hysteria to lock up "felons", Americans were duped by corrupt politicians into building and maintaining the largest prison system in the world...few politicians had the strength to speak up and tell Americans the truth: That this would actually exacerbate, rather than correct our crime problem in America!

Almost all crime is committed by male youths ages 15 to 25, or prison recidivists from this same group, who are doing life on the installment plan. We daily turned non-violent persons into violent angry persons, by our primitive and punitive prisons, and criminal justice system. The new legislation made every effort to keep persons convicted of non-violent crimes out of our prisons, and whenever possible out of our criminal justice system.

Accordingly, There was a much greater use of "Shock" Incarceration for the first-time non-violent offender, greater use of probation, and a much greater use of "civil" probation, and the imposition of fines (both civil and criminal), in lieu of incarceration.

Indeed, incarceration was considered for use only as a last resort, not the first, as had been common in the "dark ages" in the quarter century preceding Simpson's execution. And, the taxes saved from this wasteful destructive path of trying to build our way out of our crime problem, by building more and more prisons, were spent where there should have been spent all along, in educating our youth.

Further, the new legislation included the creation of Federal Regional Diagnostic and Treatment Centers for the diagnosis and treatment of the violent offender. Violent crime can be the result of anything from the act of a pathological killer to a brain tumor, but without the proper diagnosis and treatment the public had no way of protecting itself.

The primitive notion under the "Punishment Model" (the operative model for the American Criminal Justice System, prior to this time) Equated "time in prison" as just punishment for certain crimes but under this perverse and uneven system, an offender could spend more time prison for smoking pot, than murder, and more often than any sane person could tolerate, pathological killers like McDuff, were released because they had served their "time" to kill innocent persons again!

Simple logic and wisdom confirms the truism that vengeance only begets vengeance . As a result of our archaic thinking, however, the most dangerous serial killer in America, at the time, was the State of Texas. The only correct evaluation of the "Punishment Model" is that the model, itself, is insane. Also, the new legislation provided for voluntary admissions to the Diagnostic and Treatment Centers, which was particularly helpful for youth subject to momentary feelings of violence, and in cases of domestic violence, thus these persons could seek treatment in the interest of preventing crime , without the stigma of a criminal record.

Also, long overdue, was revision of our drug prevention legislation. We had wasted billions upon billions of taxpayer's dollars on the promise that "interdiction" would solve our drug problem--and yet every knowledgeable study showed this was a "push-down, pop-up" problem, i.e., because drug sales are very lucrative, even if we did interdict and stop the flow of drugs from Columbia (for example)....a new market would soon "pop-up" in Indonesia. And, thus interdiction was never more than a Band-Aid program…and did nothing to address the systemic changes that were necessary to correct this insidious problem.

England had had particular success in treating drug addiction as a "medical", rather than as a "criminal" problem (as addictions [of all types] rightly should be treated), and England introduced a program to provide the addictive drug to the addict, and thus was able to dry up drug-related crime. Also, since marijuana grows wild in every state, and has always been impossible to control, America took the lead advanced by Australia and legalized citizen's home grown, and we also allowed the sale of marijuana in our liquor stores.

By legalizing the sale of marijuana we were better able to keep marijuana out of the hands of our youth (the same as with alcohol), As any middle school child at the time would confirm...it was ten times easier to get marijuana for a party, than liquor, because of state control.

As noted, this comprehensive legislative package became known as the Economic Inclusivism Act. For too long we had seen the destructive results of "exclusion", and how this had contributed to our insidious crime problem, and social ills.

Economic Inclusivism is probably best understood as a more modern form of capitalism, and work/training became the legal (constitutional) right of every citizen.

Integral to the Economic Inclusivism Act was job creation legislation, specifically the passage of deficit-neutral THE NEIGHBOR-TO-NEIGHBOR JOB CREATION ACT [hereafter NTN]—a federally mandated Social Insurance, owned by our employed, to provide a fund to hire/train our unemployed.

For a modest 4% of salary policy cost, we created more "private-sector" jobs in 6 months, than our previous method of job creation in 6 years.

Since WW II our job creation had been based on the erroneous belief that "the market can provide anybody wanting a job, with a job"—however, the data revealed that under this method of job creation, only ONCE since WW II had this resulted in an unemployment [hereafter UE] rate below 3%--in 1953—leaving millions jobless in its wake, and from the lack of employment our inner-cities had been turned into war zones, with 60% minority UE, and an epidemic of gun violence.

For instance, in 1978, Congress passed, and President Carter signed into law 15 USC § 3101 [currently HR 1000]—which provided us with the "legal authorization" to henceforth limit our UE rate to 3%, permanently—but until passage of the above—this law had been a throw-away by a combination of ignorance in how to implement it--and the obscene cash in our elections from the oligarchy—who didn't want American employees to have rights....

The comprehensive legislative changes cut our crime rate in half by the year 2012, and preserved our endangered constitutional freedoms, following 9-11.

The wall of klieg lights and cameras almost blinded OJ Simpson as he stepped to the podium to face the press, following his promise for a public statement earlier in the day--he spoke slowly, "I am today admitting myself into the Federal Regional Diagnostic and Treatment Center in Riverside".....

CHAPTER TWO

President Obama/Council of Economic Advisers:

Why is no one in Washington asking "Can the market provide anybody wanting a job, with a job"?

The answer is critical in our addressing the public's demand to FIX UNEMPLOYMENT [hereafter UE], and most pernicious "social" problem facing America, today....

That is, [if our objective is "solution driven"]--if the market cannot provide a solution to this problem—our choices are to enforce the "legal authorization" in Humphrey-Hawkins [hereafter HH] which would limit our unemployment to "3%"—permanently—or pretend the problem doesn't exist.....

And, sadly Washington has opted for the latter....[in part by selling the American people snake oil, i.e., that we don't need to look for an alternate employment solution, on the pretense that we have a solution—and we have stood on one foot and then the other as our UE inched downward]—

Indeed, since WW II our job creation has been based, solely, on the erroneous belief, above, with the result that only ONCE in this 70 years has the market created a UE rate below 3%--in 1953—leaving millions jobless in its wake—and by our indifference has turned our inner-cities into war zones, with 60% minority UE, and resulted in an epidemic of gun violence....

The bottom line, however, is that UE is a NO ONE WINS: The jobless lose, civility loses, and the market loses, to wit:

THE LAW OF DIMINISHED INCOME TO THE MARKET FROM UNEMPLOYMENT [hereafter D/UE LAW]

Short Definition:

3% is the zero-sum threshold above which unemployment starts substantially undermining the Market--and the loss in income to the Market is compounded exponentially with each percentage point of increase in unemployment, above 3%.

As it has turned out, our failure to FIX UNEMPLOYMENT, has not been from a lack of money, or jobs, but rather a lack of imagination....

For instance, both deficit-neutral HR 1000 [in Committee], and THE NEIGHBOR-TO-NEIGHBOR JOB CREATION ACT: A federally mandated Social Insurance, owned by our employed, to provide a fund to hire/train our unemployed--are both supported by the economic research that the "influx of lower-wage [jobs] into a community tends to raise wages for everyone else" [Washington Post 9/10/15]—and both would reduce our UE to 3%, in 6 months!

Ref: FULL EMPLOYMENT IS A PRO-MARKET CONCEPT, Amazon

Jim Green, Democrat opponent to Lamar Smith, Congress, 2000

Thank you for contacting the White House!

CHAPTER THREE

President Obama/Council of Economic Advisers:

Re: Trump's grandiose claim of job creation....

Since 1978 America has had the "legal authorization" to limit our unemployment [hereafter UE] to 3%--PERMANENTLY—but, to date, Washington has lacked the wherewithal/audacity to enforce this law—

That is, at no time going forward in the 21st Century should our UE rate exceed 3%--as a matter of law [15 USC § 3101]—

And yet, we have but a single Bill in Washington that enforces this "legal authorization"—HR 1000, in Committee....

Further, given diminishing jobs going forward—i.e., given "automation", alone--this law is INDISPENSABLE to the EFFECTIVE functioning of our 21st Century market economy. [people don't buy what we manufacture, when they are jobless—Source: Common Sense]....

And while it would appear that the solution is easy, the stumbling blocks preventing its implementation are multi-faceted:

And perhaps the first is just plain tradition—like old habits die hard...[for example, Harrison died a month after his inauguration, because "bleeding" was the treatment for pneumonia in 1841]....

And when we compound this with the Koch brothers [a metaphor, here, for the 1%] spending tens of millions since WW II buying governors/legislators to abolish Job Security for Americans—i.e., to cement "at will" employment in every state [only Montana limits to probationary employees]—and to abolish labor unions—

It is little wonder that this agenda [which dominates Washington, and smothers opposition] has resulted in 8 million currently jobless, with 60% minority UE in our inner-cities, and has turned our inner-cities into war zones, with an epidemic of gun violence......

Further, this agenda is based on the erroneous belief that "the market can provide anybody wanting a job, with a job"—when in fact this fallacious path has resulted in a UE rate below 3% only ONCE since WW II—in 1953—leaving millions jobless in its wake, and resulted in the inner-cities, above....

However, running in parallel—86% of Americans believe that "anybody wanting to work, should be able to find a job"—i.e., enforcing the above "legal authorization" has not been stalled by a lack of political will, but rather has been drowned in a sea of cash by the Koch brothers—to keep us in our place.....

Ref: FULL EMPLOYMENT IS A PRO-MARKET CONCEPT, Amazon

Jim Green, candidate for Congress, 2000

Thank you for contacting the White House!

Comments: 202-456-1111
Switchboard: 202-456-1414

CHAPTER FOUR

President Obama/Council of Economic Advisers:

It took us almost 65 years to evolve from "separate but equal", to we are "equal"—[and some are still evolving]--and the same phenomenon is at play in our inability to find a solution to unemployment—like <u>Plessy v Ferguson</u>, to the injury of millions in the process.

For instance, unemployment [hereafter UE] is the most pernicious "social" problem facing America, today, and our inability to fix has resulted in 60% minority UE in our inner-cities, with an epidemic of gun violence....

And, this is in spite of the fact that 86% of Americans believe that "anybody wanting to work should be able to find a job" [i.e., full employment has solid political support]; and, since 1978 we have had on the books the "legal authorization" to limit our UE rate to "3%" [15 USC § 3101—currently HR 1000, in Committee]--.....

The fly in the ointment—a major contributing factor--is the obscene cash driving our political agenda, i.e., with the 1% believing they are on the right path [in truth] to relegate American employees to A POOL OF SLAVES: To Be Used and Discarded "at will" [Amazon]—

And they have spent tens of millions since WW II buying governors/legislators to cement "at will" in every state [only Montana limits to probationary employees]; and to destroy unions in America!

The bottom line, however, is that unemployment is a NO ONE WINS— the jobless lose, civility loses, and the market loses, to wit:

THE LAW OF DIMINISHED INCOME TO THE MARKET FROM UNEMPLOYMENT [hereafter D/UE LAW]

Short Definition:

> 3% is the zero-sum threshold above which unemployment starts substantially undermining the Market--and the loss in income to

the Market is compounded exponentially with each percentage point of increase in unemployment, above 3%.

In short, people don't buy what we manufacture, when they are jobless....and given "automation", alone, our UE crisis is expanding in our 21 Century market economy—i.e., HR 1000 is indispensable to the effective functioning of a modern market economy!

In sum, HR 1000 is a "win-win"—the jobless win, and the market wins....

Ref: FULL EMPLOYMENT IS A PRO-MARMET CONCEPT, and THE NEIGHBOR-TO-NEIGHBOR JOB CREATION ACT, Amazon

Jim Green, Democrat opponent to Lamar Smith, Congress, 2000

Thank you for contacting the White House!

CHAPTER FIVE

President Obama:

There is nothing more important on the Brother's Keeper list than ending unemployment—mostly, because it has tentacles into the solution for all of our social issues.

Indeed, 95% of our social ills will be addressed by fixing this one problem, to wit: gun violence, prison reform, youth unemployment, our inner-cities, etc....

Since WW II the Koch brothers [both specifically, and a metaphor, here, for the 1%], have spent tens of millions buying governors/legislators to eliminate "employee rights"....

Specifically, to cement "at will" employment in every state [the abolition of Job Security]—only Montana restricts to probationary employees—and in the decimation of labor unions....

And in the latter, only this past March 9th in Wisconsin, the "right to work" laws [a misnomer on steroids] crossed the 50% mark, with the goal of the Republicans in Congress to install this union busting law in the remaining 25 states!

In short, we are moving 180 degrees in the wrong direction—and driving this is the false and pernicious belief/propaganda that "the market can provide anybody wanting a job, with a job"....

With the result that only ONCE since WW II has this belief/path resulted in an unemployment rate below 3%--in 1953—leaving millions jobless in its wake and it has perpetuated the current epidemic of gun violence in our inner-cities....

Further, given "automation", alone, our unemployment crisis is being exacerbated with each passing year in the 21st Century.

In 1978, Humphrey and Hawkins [a former VP, and first black 3) Election officials assigned to oversee the EVM, would be prevented by law from overseeing the OS, and vice-versa, and stiff criminal penalties would be imposed for violations. legislator from California] provided us with the blueprint for Job Creation in our 21st Century economy—[15 USC § 3101]---but for the most part, this law has been misunderstood.

Mostly, because it not only addresses our Brother's Keeper—it is a Pro-Market solution, and indeed, it is indispensable to the effective functioning of a modern market economy [and the flaw in ignoring extends to the OECD].

Congressman Conyers has picked up the torch in implementing this 21st Century solution [HR 1000, in Committee]—

And, the purpose of this letter is to urge your support in getting this law [concept] implemented.

With highest regards,

Jim Green, Democrat opponent to Lamar Smith, Congress, 2000

CHAPTER SIX

Ras Baraka, Mayor of Newark, NJ

95% of our social ills would by addressed—including gun violence, youth unemployment, etc., by the passage of HR 1000.

A brief history....the "I had a dream" speech in 1963 was primarily about JOBS.

After Dr. King's death—civil rights leaders, including Jesse Jackson, marched on his birthday for the passage of job creation legislation—

And, finally in 1978 President Carter signed into law Humphrey-Hawkins [15 USC § 3101], which provided us with the "legal authorization" to limit our unemployment [hereafter UE] rate to 3%--permanently.

It was one of the most important pieces of legislation in the 20th Century—but neo-liberals have done everything, since, to prevent its implementation—and in the process have turned our inner-cities into war zones, with an epidemic of gun violence.

Further, given automation, alone—the problem is exacerbated with each passing year in the 21st Century.

As a result of the above, our current job creation is based on the erroneous belief that "the market can provide anybody wanting a job, with a job"—but on this path only ONCE since WWII has this resulted in a UE rate below 3%--in 1953—leaving millions jobless in its wake, and created our inner-cities, above.

The over-arching point is that on our current path we cannot create enough jobs—and it appears that until we break the neo-liberal fear of public-sector jobs—the adverse consequence of UE will persist.

Unemployment is a "social" problem—i.e., we, as the larger society, have the absolute responsibility to address—and 86% of Americans believe that "anybody wanting to work should be able to find a job"—it is not the lack of political will standing in the way.

The bottom line, however, is that UE is a NO ONE WINS—the unemployed lose, civility loses, and the market loses—people do not buy what we manufacture, when they are jobless.

There are various deficit-neutral methods to implement the "reservoir of public employees" authorized under HH—Congressman Conyers has picked up the torch with HR 1000—similarly, is The Neighbor-To-Neighbor Job Creation Act [Amazon]: a federally mandated Social Insurance, owned by our employed, to provide a fund to hire/train our unemployed.

Jim Green, Democrat candidate for Congress, 2000

Bio info: http://www.am00azon.com/James-L.-Jim-Green/e/B001KHZIMM/ref=ntt_dp_epwbk_0

CC: President Obama

CHAPTER SEVEN

President Obama/Council of Economic Advisers:

Two-thirds of the world's 7 billion population live in market-driven economies—1.2 billion are in the OECD, with China and India, alone, adding an additional 2.6 billion, and anyone who doesn't think China is a market economy, hasn't shopped at Wal-Mart....

The over-arching point, here, is the unwritten, but nevertheless pervasive/pernicious belief in our market-driven economies is that "the market can provide anybody wanting a job, with a job"....it is pernicious because it causes the "rank and file" to oppose climate change—in their belief that this is their *ONLY* means to get a Job! And, when, in fact, it is *BS, NOT* supported by the data or empirical evidence....

With the result that our record in job creation is deplorable—i.e., this methodology is woefully inadequate, as we inch along, and 5 years after the declared end of the Great Recession—we still have almost 10 million jobless Americans....

The question *NOT* being asked in Washington is: How do we address our pernicious unemployment in America—when the market cannot create enough jobs?

Had we put a lawnmower engine in the Saturn V rocket, on our Apollo 11 trip to the moon—we would never have gotten there...a perfect metaphor for our current method of job creation in America—which leaves millions jobless for years—and skewed against minorities.....

The fact is, *ONLY ONCE* in the past 65 years—under our "market only job creation" model—has our unemployment rate dropped below "3%"—in 1953—and in spite of the "legal authorization" in the U.S., since 1978, to limit our unemployment to 3% [15 USC § 3101].

In short, at *NO* time since 1978, and to this day, should our unemployment rate in America exceed 3% [HR 1000]---when, in fact, our jobless rate, today, is double that—and it will be 2017 before we return to even an anemic 5.5%, as projected by the CBO--

And the irony is that unemployment is a "NO ONE WINS" proposition—both the jobless lose, and the market loses, to wit:

> 3% is the zero-sum threshold above which unemployment starts substantially undermining the Market--and the loss in income to the Market is compounded exponentially with each percentage point of increase in unemployment, above 3%.

> FULL EMPLOYMENT IS A PRO-MARKET CONCEPT
> [Amazon]

Jim Green, Democrat opponent to Lamar Smith, Congress, 2000

CHAPTER EIGHT

President Obama/Council of Economic Advisers:

A German-national advised—in response to a question perplexing me for years—"Why on earth did the German people, with their rich cultural history, fall under the spell of a monster like Hitler"? And without a moments hesitation he said "Because he put them to work".

There is a message in there of vital importance: The value humans place on being a productive member of society—the value we place on "work"—even raising the question if it should become a Human Right?

And while giving lip service to the plight of the unemployed--our market economies, the OECD, which includes the U.S., all suffer from high unemployment—and none address unemployment as a "social" problem—with serious social consequences--WE, as a society have the RESPONSIBILITY to address—Rather they leave the creation of employment up to the whims of the market--And if the market fails, the unemployed are out of luck!

Which raises the question: The market suffers when people are unemployed—and the unemployed suffer when they are not working—so WHY on earth do our market-driven economies continue down such an unrewarding--a lose-lose path—where the market loses, and the unemployed lose?

The late Peter Drucker advocated for CEO salaries being limited to 20 times that of the lowest paid employee [the Swiss recently had on the ballot 12 times]—but it is argued that a brain-drain would occur if we didn't leave this to the market to set CEO salaries—

And whether or not this is true—WHY on earth do we persist in the anachronistic BELIEF that the market can provide anybody wanting a job, with a job [untrue since the mid-1970's]--particularly, and given automation, alone--an expanding and contracting public workforce is an INDISPENSABLE component to the EFFECTIVE functioning of a modern market economy?

Indeed, in the U.S. we have the "legal authority" on the books [15 USC § 3101], to limit our unemployment to 3%--in short, at no time should our unemployment exceed 3%--So why does Washington avoid this legal authority as if it were the plague—such as indifference to deficit—neutral solutions, i.e., HR 870, or via Social Insurance in The Neighbor-To-Neighbor Job Creation Act?

Please see: WHY WE CAN'T FIX UNEMPLOYMENT, Amazon

Highest regards,

Jim Green, Democrat opponent to Lamar Smith, Congress, 2000

CHAPTER NINE

President Obama/Council of Economic Advisers:

Capitalism is ideal in producing and selling corn flakes and cars—It doesn't work in solving "social problems" such as unemployment and our healthcare....

And when we have tried "privatization" to solve our social problems—it has been a disaster:

Essential programs have been cut—such as the elimination of text books from the Job Corps education program—to increase profits, and cronyism has run rampant—

And in our "for profit" healthcare system, billions of dollars are siphoned away from the premiums we send in—and do not go to the healthcare of ANYONE—but rather is used to pay for lobbyists, to make the CEO's filthy rich—and spent on propaganda ads to keep it that way!

Further, it attracts a few who see healthcare as a means to get rich, rather than cure the ill....

The truth is, we currently have a blended system—and they are, in fact, indispensable to each other:

Were it not for Social Security Insurance moneys percolating up through our economy in 2008—we would not be talking about having narrowly averted another Great Depression—We would be buried in one!

Social Insurance is a vital ingredient in building a vibrant and decent society—And, invent a better widget, sell the company for a million bucks, and retire in South Florida [capitalism]—is as well a vital ingredient in building a vibrant and decent society.

So why do we have this war of words pitting the two against each other—rather than educating the American people regarding the indispensable symbiotic relationship they have to each other?

Were it not for the $2 trillion + Washington infuses into the economy annually—capitalism would fold in a NY Second!

And yet, most Republicans ask God in their prayers at night to be protected from becoming communists, or socialists, or even worse "liberals"—i.e., ignorant of what the terms mean…..

And this war of words disguises that the Republican Party, today, is not the Pro-Market party they boast—but rather their policies are, in fact, Anti-Market—destructive to capitalism!

Pandering to the GREED of their wealthiest contributors—the Republican One and Only program—is NOT a Pro-Market concept!

Another misnomer in the war of words, is right-wing invented "entitlement"—a word that should be banned from honest discussion—do we refer to our auto insurance as an "entitlement"?

And when Social Security Insurance brings in more that it pays out, i.e., is deficit-neutral--how is that an "entitlement", and why is it portrayed in our graphs as a "government expense"—or even included in these graphs? If a corporation reported a massive loss on a product they in fact made money—they would be charged with fraud in a New York Minute!

The list goes on—please see: OUR GREED AND IGNORANCE, on Amazon/Kindle

Jim Green, Democrat congressional opponent to Lamar Smith, 2000

CHAPTER TEN

President Obama/Council of Economic Advisers:

THE HISTORY OF HUMPHREY-HAWKINS

The historic March On Washington, and Dr. King's "I had a dream" speech, in 1963, was a march for JOBS.

At that time, and to this day, our job creation in America has been based on the premise that "the market can provide anybody wanting a job, with a job—

And yet, only ONCE since WW II has this method of job creation resulted in an unemployment rate below 3%--in 1953—leaving millions jobless in its wake.

Following Dr. Kings death in 1968, civil rights leaders, including Jesse Jackson, annually marched on Dr. King's birthday for legislation that would address our pervasive unemployment in America.

Their demand was not without legal foundation. In 1946, President Truman signed into law the [FULL] EMPLOYMENT ACT OF 1946, to provide employment for our troops returning from WW II.

The 1%, however, balked at American employees having rights— particularly a right to employment [the model which exists to this day]—and the law was never implemented.

Ironically, Australia enacted a law similar to President Truman's Employment Act—and for the same reason—and for the next 30 years [and until the ill-winds of neo-liberalism in the mid-1970's] Australia's employment model was based on the premise that "anybody wanting to work should be able to find a job"—with 2% or less unemployment common. Australians still refer to this as their "Golden Age".

As a result of the demand by civil rights leaders for legislation, however, in 1978 President Carter signed into law—what is commonly known as the Humphrey-Hawkins Full Employment Act [15 USC § 3101].

The law provides the "legal authorization" for the creation of a "reservoir of public employees" anytime our unemployment in America exceeds "3%". That is, and to this day—at no time should our unemployment rate in America exceed 3%.

The money in politics, however, has prevented this law from being implemented!

Notwithstanding, a lone Congressman, Conyers [and a growing number of co-sponsors] has diligently worked to implement Humphrey-Hawkins [currently, deficit-neutral HR 1000, in Committee].

And, singularly, unemployment is the most pernicious problem facing America, today....

Ref: FULL EMPLOYMENT IS A PRO-MARKET CONCEPT, Amazon

Jim Green, Democrat opponent to Lamar Smith, 2000

Thank You!
Thank you for contacting the White House.

CHAPTER ELEVEN

President Obama:

It is impossible to reform our broken criminal justice system—absent our creating a viable job creation program in America.

And while it is generally believed that we do have a job creation program, in fact, we do not!

We have the BELIEF that "the market can provide anybody wanting a job, with a job"—but the data shows that only ONCE since WW II has this belief resulted in an unemployment rate below 3%--in 1953—leaving millions jobless in its wake-- and has resulted in:

60% minority unemployment in our inner-cities, with drug economies, and an epidemic of homicides [i.e., not fixing unemployment has turned our inner-cities into war zones, and created a breeding ground for our inexplicable incarceration rate].

Further this "belief" has been a stumbling block in finding a solution for our pervasive unemployment--In short, we have not been looking for a solution—because our policy makers believe we have one—and apparently few have looked at the data….

Also, ignored in the discussion is that unemployment is a "social" problem, with adverse, and oft severe social consequences—both for the individual, as well as the larger society [i.e., it is the responsibility of the larger society to solve]—

With tentacles integral to all of the social problems facing Americans, today—for instance, ending unemployment is integral to Criminal Justice Reform, and the repair of our crumbling infrastructure….

Further, in 1975 we spent $5 educating our youth, for every $1 we spent on prisons…..by the mid-1990's [with the American people having been terrorized by the Willie Horton ad—and on an hysterical prison building spree] our competing tax dollars tipped in favor of prisons—and at present we spend more on prisons, than on educating our youth.

The irony in all of this is that we have the "legal authorization", on the books to reduce our unemployment rate to 3%, tomorrow [15 USC § 3101—and deficit-neutral HR 1000, currently in Committee]—and also ignored in this context, is that President Obama had a weapon in addressing our economic meltdown in 2008, not available to FDR—and that is the $800 billion in Social Security Insurance claims percolating up through our economy—and in the absence of which--We would be buried in another Great Depression!

Turning the page—and given "automation", alone, is critical going forward in the 21st Century—and is a "win-win"—the American people win, and the market wins....

Ref: FULL EMPLOYMENT IS A PRO-MARKET CONCEPT, Amazon

Jim Green, Democrat opponent to Lamar Smith, 2000

CHAPTER TWELVE

President Obama/Council of Economic Advisers:

Our network of market-driven economies [the OECD, including the U.S]—currently have a pernicious job creation modality—with resulting high and pervasive unemployment since the mid-1970's—and on a collision course with the future—i.e., given "automation", alone, fewer and fewer jobs are being created with each passing year, as we advance into the 21st Century....

This job creation modality is based on the erroneous propaganda/belief that "the market can provide anybody wanting a job, with a job"—and yet, only ONCE since WW II has this modality resulted in an unemployment rate below 3%--in 1953—leaving millions jobless in its wake, and has resulted in our inner-cities turning into war zones--with 60% minority unemployment, drug economies, and an epidemic of homicides.

The irony in this disaster, however, is that the U.S. correctly anticipated this result in 1978—and provided the American people with a solution, i.e., the "legal authorization" [15 USC § 3101] to limit our unemployment henceforth to "3%", and as we advance into the 21st Century—

With a ton of cash poured into our political system, and a mind-set with both feet planted on the plantation—--special interests sabotaged this law to prevent its implementation—to the detriment of Americans, and America [ISIS is the least of our worries in America, when we have the Republican party]!

Unemployment is a "social" problem, with adverse social consequences....it is solely the province of the larger society to solve—and leaving the solution to anything as erratic as the market—as we do now—is patently absurd!

The bottom line is that unemployment is a NO ONE WINS....the jobless lose, civility loses, and the market loses, to wit:

THE LAW OF DIMINISHED INCOME TO THE MARKET FROM UNEMPLOYMENT [hereafter D/UE LAW]

3% is the zero-sum threshold above which unemployment triggers inflation by diminishing labor training and skills, under-utilizing capital resources, reducing the rate of productivity advance, increasing unit labor costs, reducing the general supply of goods and services--and the loss in income to the Market is compounded exponentially with each percentage point of increase in unemployment, above 3%.

Ref: HR 1000 [in Committee], and FULL EMPLOYMENT IS A PRO-MARKET SOLUTION, Amazon

Jim Green, Democrat opponent to Lamar Smith, 2000

Thank You!

Thank you for contacting the White House

THE HISTORY OF HOW WE GOT WHERE WE ARE
[WW II to Present]

Following WW II, President Truman signed into law the [FULL] EMPLOYMENT ACT of 1946, to provide employment for our returning troops.

Ironically, half-way around the world, Australia codified into their law an almost identical Bill, and for the same reason—

Difference is—Australia actually put their law into effect, and over the next 30 years it was intrinsic to employment policy in Australia that "anybody wanting to work should be able to find a job"—and save for a brief recession in 1961/62 their unemployment was 2%, or less. This period is still referred to as their "Golden Age", in Australia.

Unforeseen by either country, however, in the mid-1970's the world economy underwent a major paradigm shift as a result of the colliding forces of automation, globalization, technology, etc., reaching a critical mass—in brief, an adjustment towards modernity—From a perverse perspective, we became victims of our success....

The instability caused by this transition, however, resulted in a malaise, and ushered in the ill-winds of greed-driven neo-liberalism with its indifference to unemployment, and the likes of Thatcher and Reagan— and the menace of this greed-driven agenda was exploded by Bush II, resulting in obscene disparities in wealth that persists, and is the cause of much friction between right and left, to this day.

It also ushered in high and pervasive unemployment throughout our market-driven economies, the OECD—with 6% unemployment in

Australia now the norm, and double-digit unemployment common throughout the Eurozone, to this day.

As a result of the "malaise", however, the U.S. took an aggressive, pro-active role in addressing the, above, economic shift—and in 1978 President Carter signed into law one of the most important laws in the 20th Century--an expansion of President Truman's full employment, i.e., Pro-Market 15 USC § 3101--which provides a "*legal authorization*" to create a "reservoir of public employees" [*indispensable to the effective functioning of a 21st Century market economy*]--at any time our unemployment in America exceeds "3%"—

But in spite of 3% unemployment being the threshold point above which unemployment starts substantially undermining the Market—this *legal authorization* has never been implemented--

And in spite of deficit-neutral HR 1000, or The Neighbor-To-Neighbor Job Creation Act—A federally mandated Social Insurance, owned by our employed, to provide a fund to hire/train our unemployed—[more on the critical need to apply this job creation methodology in a 21st Century market economy, ahead]….

Ref: FULL EMPLOYMENT IS A PRO-MARKET CONCEPT, Amazon/Kindle

Jim Green, Democrat opponent to Lamar Smith, Congress, 2000

CHAPTER FOURTEEN

THE HISTORY OF HOW WE GOT WHERE WE ARE
[Mid-1970's to Present]

In the mid-1970's, the colliding forces of automation, technology, globalization, etc., reached a critical mass—resulting in a Market no longer capable of producing the jobs necessary to its viability, and causing ubiquitous unemployment in all of the OECD countries—and leaving their leaders conflicted, ever since, regarding the displaced employee. Eurozone unemployment is still in double digits, and Greece and Spain both in excess of 20%, plus. High unemployment was also a major factor in Arab Spring.

In the U.S., we took a pro-active role in addressing this economic shift—and in 1978 President Carter signed into law 15 USC § 3101--which "authorizes" the creation of a "reservoir of public employment" at any time our unemployment in America exceeds "3%".

In 1979, however, and in a panic over Humphrey-Hawkins—our ultra-conservative foundations, and desperate to promote the Supply-Side fraud, embraced a flawed paper by an obscure MIT student, David L. Birch "The Job Generation Process"; and [with lots of cash] gave his paper biblical importance, and every president since has cited his finding as gospel.

Birch's paper concluded that "small businesses" were the greatest generator of new jobs—problem is, for the purposes of policy-making—it is BS. In a study at Harvard University in 2010, "The Myth of Small Business Job Creation" The research shows "no systematic relationship between firm size and growth." And that small businesses can actually detract from job growth.

In spite of this, however, Washington struggles, still, to make this antiquated notion, work--that it is only the market that can create jobs—and the result has been a disaster, politically as well as otherwise!

It would be impossible to still have 7.8% unemployment—if we were on the right path—and among other problems with this concept--if the market fails, the unemployed are out of luck.

Further, unemployment is a "social" problem we are seeking to address with a highly unstable, incompatible entity: The Market

What apparently isn't clear going forward is that an expanding and contracting public workforce is an *indispensable* component to the *effective* functioning of a modern market economy—

The market thrives when we have a robust, employed, consuming workforce—and overlooked is that HR 1000 [currently in Committee], and the proposed "Neighbor-To-Neighbor Job Creation Act" www.Inclusivism.org [both authorized under Humphrey-Hawkins], are deficit-neutral--Pro-Market "win-win" solutions:

The American people win, and capitalism wins—

Jim Green, Democrat candidate for Congress, 2000

CHAPTER FIFTEEN

Friends: In the event you have gotten this far—according to the Federal Election Commission, I am a candidate for president in the 2016 election—and rest assured I am not delusional, or like Trump…on an ego trip…..I filed solely to deliver a message—you are reading it—and to urge passage of the above legislation….

To Whom It May Concern—in Washingon:

OUR CHOICES ARE: Adapt and change in a world that is changing, whether we like it or not, OR be forced to create a Police State to hold our anachronistic policies, practices and laws in place—

And in America, today, we have chosen the latter…..and as only one pernicious example, of thousands—Ferguson is the result….

In a comedic, but religious context we hear of persons asking God for a sign—anything—which will warn us that we are on the wrong path, and need to change direction…..and our Police State choice, above, is *our sign*…..few are listening….

To illustrate a critical area in which we need to adapt and change in a 21st Century economy: We have far more work that needs to be done in America, than we have persons to fill these jobs—And 86% of Americans believe that "Anybody wanting to work should be able to find a job"---So, why on earth *in a democracy*, do we have 9 million jobless Americans—[per the 11/14 DOL Jobs report]?

The answer is because our *method* of job creation in America is based on a Fairy Tale! Specifically, our current *one and only* job creation methodology in America, is based on the myth/sacred cow:

"The market can provide anybody wanting a job, with a job"—

Problem is—it is pure BS—and only *once* since WW II has this methodology resulted in an unemployment rate below 3%--in 1953 [i.e., which translates into 5 million left jobless]--because the market *cannot* create enough jobs—in short, the jobs for this 5 million jobless--*don't exist*!

The right-wing propaganda mills trick our fools into believing that the market has created this 5 million jobs, but because those on welfare are "lazy and don't want to work" this 5 million jobs go unfilled—but that is *pure balderdash!*

The vast majority of persons on welfare, are there *because* the *market* cannot create enough jobs, i.e., the market lacks the viability to create these jobs—the jobs simply *do not exist*!

And as further proof, according to the CBO, on our current path it will be 2017 before America returns to even an anemic 5.5% unemployment rate [following the Great Recession] and if the market fails in the interim—the jobless are out of luck!

Further, this travesty is compounded because the Republicans cling to devious and discredited Supply Side Economics [to this day] as a solution, to wit:

Siphon America's wealth away from the consuming middle—give this windfall of cash to the Koch Bros [a metaphor for the 1%, hereafter "KB"]—they will build factories all across our fair land—everyone will have a job in the corporation—and we will all live happily ever after— Yes, folks it is a fairy tale!

And what we learned from this dark cloud over America is what Bush I called it long ago—before America was subjected to this devious scam— i.e., Supply-Side is "VooDoo Economics"!

So why have we allowed ourselves to be deceived by this Republican scam—[handcrafted by a plutocracy/oligarchy that still has one foot on the plantation]? But I don't want to giveaway the surprise ending—and some of my response isn't printable....! Further, and to say it up front....I am a capitalist—I support 100%: Build a better widget, sell it for a million bucks, and retire in South Florida....it is the Republican agenda, today, that is anti-market...more on this throughout.....

When President Carter handed the reigns over to Reagan in 1981—he left America with a very modest $60 billion deficit—as a direct result of Supply-Side, however, when Republicans held the White House [Clinton actually cut the deficit]—this $60 billion ballooned to a staggering $10 trillion by 2008—and it has cost Americans an additional $7+trillion to clean up this Republican mess—

Ask any economist: Our only way out of a meltdown *is to buy our way out!* [it was the lesson learned from the Great Depression].

And anyone who thinks McCain, had he been elected, would not have addressed this with a Stimulus, the same as President Obama in 2009—is stuffed between the cars with rice pudding......

Further, we learned that we cannot siphon America's wealth away from the consuming middle, and give it to the "KB"—without sending our economy into meltdown—as occurred in 1987 and 2008—in short, the Supply-Side scam has a shelf-life of about 7 years before the economy collapses—and as noted, costing the taxpayers trillions to put a floor under a disappearing economy!

And another fallout/direct result from this dark chapter is the disparity in wealth it has created in America—AKA the "wealth gap"--and currently the "richest 1 percent in the United States now own more wealth than the bottom 90 percent"—the second highest in our history, the first was just before the Great Depression.

A couple of other factors that played into the above scenario—when every waking moment in capitalism is spent pondering how to eliminate as many of us humans, as possible, from the workplace—to increase "profits"—why, on Earth, would we look to the market to solve our unemployment crisis in America?

As well, few things on earth are more unstable than the market....we can count on one hand the number of corporations in America that were around in 1900....with tens of thousands long since disappeared; and given "automation", alone, the market will produce fewer and fewer jobs the further we advance into the 21st Century.

Further, unemployment is a "social" problem—we, as the larger society have the responsibility to solve—i.e., it is unrealistic to expect the market to solve this problem—the market is in the "for profit" business, not the social work business—and the former would not long be in business--if they were...for example, we should never condemn the CEO for closing a plant when they are losing money—but we should be outraged by a government that doesn't have a clue re the displaced employees......

Also, unemployment is a _no one wins_ .....the jobless lose, and market loses, to wit:

3% is the zero-sum threshold above which unemployment triggers inflation by diminishing labor training and skills, under-utilizing capital resources, reducing the rate of productivity advance, increasing unit labor costs, and reducing the general supply of goods and services--and the loss in income to the Market is compounded exponentially with each percentage point of increase in unemployment, above 3%.

Short Definition:

3% is the zero-sum threshold above which unemployment starts substantially undermining the Market--and the loss in income to the Market is compounded exponentially with each percentage point of increase in unemployment, above 3%.

In sum, our job creation should be based on: Fix unemployment, and this will fix the market [HR 1000], rather than [our current mind-set] Fix the market, and this in turn fix unemployment [HR 2847] – with a result that has been a disaster—as we inch along in our job recovery, see data above, and when we didn't _Fix Unemployment_ a retaliatory electorate ushered in a House filled with lunatics in the 2010 election, and then doubled down in 2014!

Look around—all signs in our economy are up—and yet over two-thirds of our rank and file believe "we are moving in the wrong direction"—

their perception is that our economy is in the tank—that we are in an economic malaise—a condition that would disappear overnight if we did, in fact, *Fix Unemployment*!

Best guess is that Congress passed, and President Obama signed into law HR 2847 [the HIRE Act], in 2009—which is based on fix the market, and this will fix unemployment [180 degrees off course]—but they did this because of the pervasive [but false] *belief* that "The market can provide anybody wanting a job, with a job"—it is *pure BS……it doesn't work*! Had we insisted on putting a lawnmower engine in the rocket to get us to the Moon….we would never have gotten there…[same difference]….and all of the empirical evidence is proof HR 2847 didn't create anywhere near the jobs needed…

Jim Green, Democrat opponent to Lamar Smith, Congress, 2000

CHAPTER SIXTEEN

HOPPER-READY: THE NEIGHBOR-TO-NEIGHBOR JOB CREATION ACT

[1] PROPOSED LEGISLATION:

THE NEIGHBOR-TO-NEIGHBOR JOB CREATION ACT

A Pro-Market, deficit-neutral, federally mandated, Social Insurance, owned by our employed, to provide a fund to hire/train our unemployed.

SECTION 1. SHORT TITLE.

This Act shall be cited as The Neighbor-To-Neighbor Job Creation Act [To establish employment/training opportunities for the unemployed in compliance with the "Legal Authorization" in Public Law 15 USC § 3101, for the creation of a "reservoir of public employees", anytime our unemployment rate exceeds "3%", with an emphasis on training for market needs, including a training stipend, where there is a shortage of trained workers--hereafter NTN].

SEC. 2. DEFINITIONS.

In this Act the following definitions apply:
(1) SECRETARY- The term `Secretary' means the Secretary of Labor.
(2) STATE- The term `State' has the meaning given such term in section 102(2) of the Housing and Community Development Act (42 U.S.C. 5302(2)).
(3) TRUST FUND- The term `Trust Fund' refers to the Department of Labor Full Employment Trust Fund.
(4) UNIT OF GENERAL LOCAL GOVERNMENT- The term `unit of general local government' has the meaning given such

term in section 102(1) of the Housing and Community Development Act (42 U.S.C. 5302(1)).

(5) URBAN COUNTY- The term `urban county' has the meaning given such term in section 102(6) of the Housing and Community Development Act (42 U.S.C. 5302(6)).

(6) WEB SITE- The Secretary shall establish an Internet Web site to serve as an information clearinghouse for job training and employment opportunities funded by the Trust Fund.

SEC. 3. EMPLOYMENT OPPORTUNITY GRANTS TO STATES, LOCAL GOVERNMENT.

(a) Use of Funds-A recipient of a grant under this section shall use the grant primarily for infrastructure repair, including, but not limited to:

(A) The painting and repair of schools, community centers, and libraries.

(B) The restoration and revitalization of abandoned and vacant properties to alleviate blight in distressed and foreclosure-affected areas of a unit of general local government.

(C) The augmentation of staffing in Head Start, child care, and other early childhood education programs to promote school readiness and early literacy.

(D) The renovation and enhancement of maintenance of parks, playgrounds, and other public spaces.

Respectfully Submitted,

Jim Green, Democrat candidate for Congress, Dist 21, TX, 2000

CHAPTER SEVENTEEN

WHAT WE NEED TO DO GOING FORWARD IN THE 21ST CENTURY:

Inexplicably "public employment" is seen the same as WPA—where millions are employed directly by the federal government—when that model is not only outmoded—it is insufficient to address our problems in the 21st century.

What we need today is an expanding and contracting public workforce—that expands during downturns in the market, and contracts as employees return to the private sector [Google: The Buffer Stock Employment Model]—triggered anytime our unemployment exceeds "3%" [as "authorized" under Humphrey-Hawkins]--and least understood: This is an INDISPENSABLE component in the effective functioning of our 21st Century Market.

The market thrives when we have a robust, employed, consuming workforce—our manufacturers are sitting on $2 trillion in cash because they do not have consumers for their products—i.e., absent consumers, they lay off employees—[and the Republican solution, Reaganomics, has acted as an accelerate to this downward spiral—and which Romney promises to return us to if he is elected]!

In short, the above model is a "win-win" solution—the American people win, and capitalism wins!

To achieve this, what is being urged is "The Neighbor-To-Neighbor Job Creation Act": A federally mandated, mutual insurance—owned by our employed [from janitor to CEO] to create a fund to hire/train our unemployed.

To be viable, however, our job creation solution _MUST_ contain:

1] Be based on the premise that we have far more work that needs to be done in America, than we have persons to fill these jobs.

2] It MUST have renewable funding.

3] It will not add a dime to our deficit.

To expand briefly, it is currently believed, erroneously, that we need "make work" jobs so that everyone who wants to work will have a job—but this is absurd—and an insult to "Yankee Ingenuity".

We do not have an unemployment crisis from a shortage of jobs, or money—but rather from a shortage of imagination.

Regarding "renewable funding" ALL of our job creation solutions, to date, have been based on the mind-set: "jump start" the market, and the market will in turn create all the jobs we need—and even setting aside that this is untrue, our current job creation is moving at a snail's pace—long past the unemployment benefits drying up—with the CBO projecting that even with the JOBS Act, signed into law on April 6, 2012--it will be 2017 before we return to a barely acceptable 5.5% unemployment rate!

Further, by its nature when we "jump start" --the employment ends when the funding runs out as we learned from the Stimulus—whereas any real fix to our unemployment crisis _demands_ renewable funding....

And whether the electorate will accept an unemployment rate hovering around 8% on election day—is the $64,000 question....

Regarding not adding a dime to our deficit—under The Neighbor-To-Neighbor Job Creation Act [NTN], the _funding_ to reduce our unemployment to 3% comes from an insurance owned by our employed, rather than added to our deficit—

If one is employed in America, participation in this insurance plan is mandatory—similar in concept to our auto insurance or Social Security Insurance [and without question the most successful social program in American history].

Jobs beget jobs--And with a modest policy cost of 4% of salary we can create more "private-sector" jobs in 6 months, that HR 2847, and the JOBS Act, in 6 years—and unlike these laws—NTN will not add a dime to our deficit!

Finally, this is in total concert with the will of the American people, i.e., that "anybody willing to work should be able to find a job"—and the American people have told our politicians time and again of their willingness to chip in to help their neighbor get a job [and as an _insurance_, as above, it also protects their continued employment]—it is just that Washington is deaf as an adder!

CHAPTER EIGHTEEN

President Obama/Council of Economic Advisers:

Public-Sector jobs strengthen our free-enterprise market economy—i.e., they are a critical component to the viability of our 21st Century economy--rather than weakening the market--as propagandist, with one foot on the plantation, fraudulently deceive the public into believing for the purposes of exploiting American employees.....

Indeed, since WW II, the Koch brothers [both literally, and a metaphor, here, for the 1%] have spent tens of millions buying governors and legislators, to cement "at will" employment in every state [and currently only Montana limits to probationary employees]; and to destroy "collective bargaining", i.e., unions in America—

In sum, they have spent tens of millions of dollars to destroy "employee rights" in America!

To understand the importance of "collective bargaining" for employees, it is informative to take a page from history:

When Hitler became the dictator in Germany, one of his first laws was to make it illegal for more than three persons to gather on the street— and German citizens were subject to immediate arrest if they did.

The same principal is being used by preventing employees putting their heads together, as it were, to bargain for employee rights—and recently one group of employees placed "job security" over a salary increase— with the irony being that the specific objective of "at will" employment—is to destroy "job security"!

In short, the deceptive propaganda to frighten Americans regarding "public-sector" jobs, has but a single parent: To exploit American labor—by some, to assuage deep-seated feelings of inferiority [they can only feel tall, by making others small, in their eyes]--—but most often for just pure GREED!

Where our policies makers go wrong by pandering to some in the oligarchy—and/or buying into this fraudulent propaganda:

Unemployment is a NO ONE WINS—the jobless lose, civility loses, and the market loses, to wit:

THE LAW OF DIMINISHED INCOME TO THE MARKET FROM UNEMPLOYMENT [hereafter D/UE LAW]

Short Definition:

> 3% is the zero-sum threshold above which unemployment starts substantially undermining the Market--and the loss in income to the Market is compounded exponentially with each percentage point of increase in unemployment, above 3%.

Ref: IT IS IMPOSSIBLE TO BE A CHRISTIAN, AND VOTE REPUBLICAN, Amazon

Jim Green, Democrat opponent to Lamar Smith, 2000

CHAPTER NINETEEN

I didn't write the following. It is a cut and paste from FACEBOOK, or some blog [would like to give credit if knew the author]--but it is so on target regarding how "fear" is driving Conservative policy in America today—i.e., is undermining America and our progress—and relegating America to a Third World country status, rather than a world leader— FDR had it on the nose in "All we have to fear, is fear itself"…at his inaugural in 1933….

"Conservatives are such cowards: they are afraid of gay people getting married or serving in the military; they are afraid of bringing terrorists to super max prisons in the US from which no one has ever escaped; they are afraid of the boy scouts letting gay kids in; they are afraid of everyone voting and are constantly suppressing the vote under some bogus voter fraud theory; they are afraid of letting students vote at their universities; they are afraid of women having the right to choose; they even are afraid of women getting contraception [the real issue actually is a women's agency and control over their bodies]; they are afraid of immigration reform leading to citizenship because they are afraid of-- name whatever reason; they are afraid of mandating gun purchasers to undergo background checks for crazy people and terrorists; they are afraid of people smoking pot; they are afraid of climate change being real and contradicting their beloved Bible; they are afraid of legitimate campaign reform; they are afraid of Muslims; they are afraid of blacks; they are afraid of atheists; they are afraid of hippies; they are afraid of socialists; they are probably still afraid of monsters under their beds; they are just rank cowards and keep making things up to be afraid of."

CHAPTER TWENTY

[I couldn't resist including this…and yes I am the author…..]

A MESSAGE FROM GOD

MANY CENTURIES AGO, a man of the cloth, we don't know his name, and in a flash of insight (perhaps induced by peyote) told his flock that "sex is a sin". And lo and behold he learned that by taking a very natural and healthy part of our life and turning it into something that was "dirty and nasty", that he could imprison his flock, and fill his coffers, and hallelujah it was a great day for the Lord!

Quickly, his miracle spread to other churches in his village, and then to the next village, and then the next county, and then state, and soon it spread to all the churches in the ancient world, and all of their flocks cowed in fear and shame and became imprisoned, and their coffers over-floweth. Hallelujah, it was a great day for the Lord!

And to keep the myth alive they started inventing stories, half-baked stories, that made no sense to anyone who is rational, such as "Mary was a virgin"—well, she just had to be a virgin because she would never partake in anything that was dirty and nasty, like sex (if you're doing it right), and this was necessary to make "sex is a sin" make sense...so they invented a Mary that was "sinless"--you get the picture. And their coffers over-floweth. Hallelujah, it was a great day for the Lord!

No one seemed to be bothered that when we play tricks on the human mind by taking something that is very natural and healthy, such as sex, and make it dirty and nasty that all kinds of bad things happen to the human mind:

Such as most pedophiles, and most serial killers, and voting Republican, and unwarranted suicides, and most mental illness, and unwanted pregnancies. (Teens not wanting to have sex is the perversion, not the other way around, and by replacing sex education and condoms, with unrealistic "abstinence", and by using blather about "low self-esteem" to shame them into not "sinning"—We have a teen pregnancy in the U.S. twice that of England and Canada!).

But none of this mattered, because their coffers over-floweth, and Hallelujah, it is a great day for the Lord!

There is a cure--------Tell our right-wing hypocrites, who Judge, rather than "Judge not".... to shove it....

GOD

ABOUT THE AUTHOR: I was employed in our Criminal Justice System for a cumulative 20 years as a probation officer, with 5 of those years as a chief probation officer. I authored the concept of "Shock Incarceration" which became law in Kansas in 1970, and then was adopted in numerous jurisdictions in the U.S. and also spread to Europe—it is currently identified in the U.S. as "Boot Camp" [as the means to "shock" the young offender—and a total distortion of my original intent—like many ideas, once released, they take on a life of their own]. I also instigated establishment of the first Court Psychiatric Clinic in the U.S., in conjunction with psychiatrists from the Menninger Foundation, as a chief probation officer. Finally, I was the Democrat candidate for Congress, District 21, TX, 2000. I would most define myself as a Social Ecologist-- [albeit my degree is in Psychology]. My web page is www.Inclusivism.org –which has been on the internet since 1996.

http://www.amazon.com/James-L.-Jim-Green/e/B001KHZIMM/ref=ntt_dp_epwbk_0

\

A BRIEF ADDENDUM: When the U.S. Supreme Court denied certiorari—where the violation of my constitutional rights were obvious, and criminal negligence on the part of the government defendants in the death of our son, equally obvious—[detailed in THE HARVARD BOYS CLUB, Amazon/Kindle]--I filed a Petition for Rehearing [which is automatic]—and included the following. The Clerk of the U.S. Supreme Court called me at my work in California, and asked that I withdraw the "cartoon" [a reprint from The NEW YORKER] from my Petition. I refused on the basis of the First Amendment, and it remains in the archives at the U.S. Supreme Court [Docket #: 79-1627], to this day. The wording [not that clear] is: "Excellent, excellent. A fine blend of truths, half-truths, and blatant falsehoods".

IN THE

Supreme Court of the United States

October Term, 1979

No. 79-1627

JAMES L. GREEN,

Petitioner,

VS.

"Excellent, excellent. A fine blend of truths, half-truths, and blatant falsehoods."

OTHER BOOKS BY THIS AUTHOR ON AMAZON/KINDLE/BN:

•THE HARVARD BOYS CLUB: Hitler's Assault On Our Freedoms From His Grave

•MY LETTERS TO PRESIDENT OBAMA: Confessions Of A Compulsive Letter Writer

•OUR GREED AND IGNORANCE: Poses A Far Greater Threat To America, Than Terrorism

•LETTERS ON STEROIDS: Confessions Of A Compulsive Letter-To-The-Editor Writer

•THE FIRST TIME I HAD SEX: And, The Religious Intolerance Attack On America

•WHY PRESIDENT OBAMA LOST THE 2012 ELECTION: A Wake-Up Call

•ECONOMIC INCLUSIVISM: Neo-Capitalism/An Anthology: Inclusive pro-market solutions to our social problems

•AMERICA IS ONE SICK MF: Why Greed-Driven America Went Off The Rails....

•EVERY GIVEN SUNDAY: A Scientific Formula To Predict NFL Games

And others....http://www.amazon.com/James-L.-Jim-Green/e/B001KHZIMM/ref=ntt_dp_epwbk_0

www.ingramcontent.com/pod-product-compliance
Lightning Source LLC
Chambersburg PA
CBHW071126280526
45787CB00003B/1182